Living
REFLECTIONS

Living
REFLECTIONS

Selections from the Bible by
DAVID SCHUBERT

with photographs by
IAN MORRIS
CHRIS SPIKER

*'The word of God
is alive and active.'
(Hebrews 4:12)*

LEFT: *Red flowering gum* SPIKER

Graphic design by Graeme Cogdell

99 98 97 96 95 94 93 92 10 9 8 7 6 5 4 3 2 1

National Library of Australia Cataloguing-in-Publication entry
    {Bible. English. Today's English. Selections. 1966}.
    Living reflections: selections from the Bible.

  ISBN 0 85910 620 9.

  1. Schubert, David A. (David Arthur), 1942–

220.52

Typeset in 11 point ITC New Baskerville by Lutheran Publishing House
Colour separations by Imagecolor
Printed by Finsbury Press

Published August 1992 by Lutheran Publishing House,
205 Halifax Street, Adelaide, South Australia

PREFACE

THE BIBLE is more than a book. It is actually a collection of books, brought together over hundreds of years. It includes history and stories, prose and poetry, prophecy and praise. The books making up the Bible were written by many different authors, writing in their own styles from varying points of view to different readers. Many of these writings rank among the world's greatest literature.

But to millions of people over the centuries the Bible has been more than this. It talks about God and his relationship to human beings; even more, through the Bible people hear God himself talking to them.

LEFT: *Golden wattles, Dunolly bush, Vic*
SPIKER
UPPER RIGHT: *Ayers Rock, NT* SPIKER
LOWER RIGHT: *Arnhem Land Beach, NT*
MORRIS

UPPER LEFT: *Redman's Bluff, Grampians, Vic* SPIKER
LOWER LEFT: *Rundle Mall, Adelaide, SA* SPIKER
RIGHT: *Yellow gum forest, Bendigo, Vic* SPIKER

Christians call the Bible the Word of God, because through the human authors writing in their particular historical situations God's message is addressed to people of all times and places. This message is sometimes devastating, as it exposes and condemns our faults and failures; but the ultimate message is **good** news, as it tells of God's love and acceptance for human beings.

The key to God's message is Jesus Christ — who is also called the Word. It is because of him that God's message is finally comfort, in spite of our own inadequacies. The Bible itself says:
In the past God spoke to our ancestors many times and in many ways through the prophets, but in these last days he has spoken to us through his Son (Hebrews 1:1,2).

When we read or hear that Jesus willingly died an innocent death on a criminal's cross, God is speaking to us, declaring his rescuing love. And when we read or hear that Jesus returned to life on the third day, God is declaring that he has conquered even death for us. We receive all that God offers us when we put our trust in Jesus.

God's Word is addressed to all people. God speaks to all cultures and nations, including Australia. The beauty, the splendour, the variety, the starkness of this country are God's creation, and he calls its people into his family. God is the God of Australia's burning sun, the God of the straggling gums, the God of the cool refreshing nights and the drought-breaking rains. He is also the God of the millions of people packed in the cities, as well as those living in country towns and in the vast outback.

This book contains a selection of passages from the Bible, together with photographs of Australia. The quotations have been chosen to give an overview of the Bible's message, from the story of the creation of the world in Genesis to the vision of the new heaven and new earth in Revelation. Favourite passages have been included, and also some that may not be as well known. The translation is the popular and readable *Good News Bible*.

David Schubert

I N THE beginning, when God created the universe, the earth was formless and desolate. The raging ocean that covered everything was engulfed in total darkness, and the power of God was moving over the water. Then God commanded, 'Let there be light' — and light appeared. God was pleased with what he saw. Then he separated the light from the darkness, and he named the light 'Day' and the darkness 'Night'. Evening passed and morning came — that was the first day.

GENESIS 1:1–5

UPPER LEFT: *Reef edge* MORRIS
LOWER LEFT: *Wet season cloud formation* MORRIS
RIGHT: *Setting sun, Nourlangie Creek, NT* MORRIS

WHEN THE LORD God made the universe, there were no plants on the earth and no seeds had sprouted, because he had not sent any rain, and there was no one to cultivate the land; but water would come up from beneath the surface and water the ground.

Then the LORD God took some soil from the ground and formed a man out of it; he breathed life-giving breath into his nostrils and the man began to live.

Then the LORD God planted a garden in Eden, in the East, and there he put the man he had formed.

GENESIS 2:4–8

LEFT: *Ground orchid* MORRIS
RIGHT: *Seasonal growth, Magela flood plain, NT* MORRIS

LEFT: *Scrub python, Daintree, Qld* MORRIS
RIGHT BACKGROUND: *Dew on spider web,
NSW* MORRIS
UPPER RIGHT: *Gums in a valley, Grampians,
Vic* SPIKER
LOWER RIGHT: *Red capped mallee* SPIKER

NOW THE snake was the most cunning animal that the LORD God had made. The snake asked the woman, 'Did God really tell you not to eat fruit from any tree in the garden?'

'We may eat the fruit of any tree in the garden', the woman answered, 'except the tree in the middle of it. God told us not to eat the fruit of that tree or even touch it; if we do, we will die.'

The snake replied, 'That's not true; you will not die. God said that because he knows that when you eat it, you will be like God and know what is good and what is bad.'

The woman saw how beautiful the tree was and how good its fruit would be to eat, and she thought how wonderful it would be to become wise. So she took some of the fruit and ate it. Then she gave some to her husband, and he also ate it. As soon as they had eaten it, they were given understanding and realised that they were naked; so they sewed fig leaves together and covered themselves.

That evening they heard the LORD God walking in the garden, and they hid from him among the trees . . .

GENESIS 3:1–8

SIN CAME into the world through one man, and his sin brought death with it. As a result, death has spread to the whole human race because everyone has sinned . . .

For sin pays its wage — death; but God's free gift is eternal life in union with Christ Jesus our Lord.

ROMANS 5:12; 6:23

UPPER LEFT: *Morning light, Fleurieu Peninsula, SA* SPIKER
LOWER LEFT: *Wild flowers, Kosciusko National Park, NSW* MORRIS
RIGHT: *The Olgas, NT* MORRIS

THE LORD said to Abram, 'Leave your country, your relatives, and your father's home, and go to a land that I am going to show you. I will give you many descendants, and they will become a great nation. I will bless you and make your name famous, so that you will be a blessing.

I will bless those who bless you, but I will curse those who curse you.
And through you I will bless all the nations.'

GENESIS 12:1–3

the God of your ancestors, the God
of Abraham, Isaac, and Jacob.' So
Moses covered his face, because he
was afraid to look at God.

Then the LORD said, 'I have seen
how cruelly my people are being
treated in Egypt . . . Now I am
sending you to the king of Egypt so
that you can lead my people out of
his country.'

EXODUS 3:1,2,5–7,10

BACKGROUND: *Sandstone fire, East Alligator
River, NT* MORRIS
LOWER RIGHT: *Stirling Ranges, WA* SPIKER

MOSES SAID: 'Israel, remember this! The LORD — and the LORD alone — is our God. Love the LORD your God with all your heart, with all your soul, and with all your strength. Never forget these commands that I am giving you today. Teach them to your children. Repeat them when you are at home and when you are away, when you are resting and when you are working. Tie them on your arms and wear them on your foreheads as a reminder. Write them on the doorposts of your houses and on your gates.'

DEUTERONOMY 6:4–9

LEFT: *Country church, south of Clare, SA* SPIKER
UPPER LEFT: *James and Natasha, Kakadu, NT* MORRIS
UPPER RIGHT: *The Olgas, NT* MORRIS

T HE LORD *said to Nathan:* 'Tell my servant David that I, the LORD Almighty, say to him, "I took you from looking after sheep in the pasture and made you the ruler of my people Israel. I have been with you wherever you have gone, and I have defeated all your enemies as you advanced. I will make you as famous as the greatest leaders in the world. I have chosen a place for my people Israel and have settled them there, where they will live without being oppressed any more. Ever since they entered this land, they have been attacked by violent people, but this will not happen again. I promise to keep you safe from all your enemies and to give you descendants. When you die and are buried with your ancestors, I will make one of your sons king and will keep his kingdom strong. He will be the one to build a temple for me, and I will make sure that his dynasty continues for ever".'

2 SAMUEL 7:8–13

LEFT: *Sheep grazing, Albany, WA* SPIKER
RIGHT: *Storm over the South Alligator River, NT* MORRIS
OVERLEAF: *Evening light, Stirling Ranges, WA* SPIKER

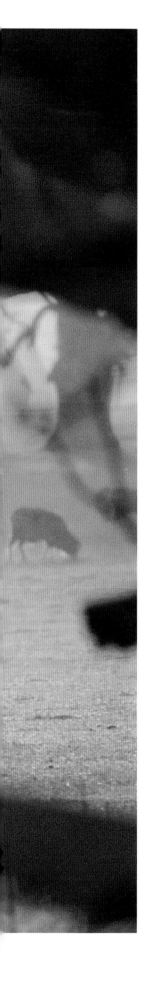

THE LORD is my shepherd;
   I have everything I need.
He lets me rest in pastures of green
      grass
   and leads me to quiet pools of
      fresh water.
He gives me new strength.
He guides me in the right paths,
   as he has promised.
Even if I go through the deepest
      darkness,
   I will not be afraid, LORD,
   for you are with me.
Your shepherd's rod and staff
      protect me.

You prepare a banquet for me,
   where all my enemies can see
      me;
you welcome me as an honoured
      guest
   and fill my cup to the brim.
I know that your goodness and love
      will be with me all my life;
   and your house will be my home
      as long as I live.

PSALM 23

LEFT: *Early morning, Naracoorte, SA* SPIKER
RIGHT: *Rainforest creek, Royal National
Park, NSW* MORRIS

G OD IS our shelter
and strength,
always ready to help
in times of trouble.
So we will not be afraid,
even if the earth is shaken
and mountains fall
into the ocean depths;
even if the seas
roar and rage,
and the hills are shaken
by the violence.

PSALM 46:1–3

B E MERCIFUL to me, O God,
because of your constant love.
Because of your great mercy
wipe away my sins!
Wash away all my evil
and make me clean from my
sin! . . .

Create a pure heart in me, O God,
and put a new and loyal spirit in
me.
Do not banish me from your
presence;
do not take your holy spirit away
from me.
Give me again the joy that comes
from your salvation,
and make me willing to obey you.

PSALM 51:1,2,10–12

UPPER LEFT: *Prince Regent River area,
Kimberleys, WA* MORRIS
LOWER LEFT: *Antilopine kangaroo,
Arnhem Land, NT* MORRIS
RIGHT: *Common ringtail, NSW* MORRIS

O LORD, you have always been our
    home.
Before you created the hills
    or brought the world into being,
    you were eternally God,
    and will be God for ever . . .

A thousand years to you are like
    one day;
    they are like yesterday, already
        gone,
    like a short hour in the night.
You carry us away like a flood;
    we last no longer than a dream.
We are like weeds that sprout in the
    morning,
    that grow and burst into bloom,
    then dry up and die in the
        evening . . .

Fill us each morning with your
    constant love,
    so that we may sing and be glad
    all our life.

PSALM 90:1,2,4–6,14

LEFT BACKGROUND: *Rock fig, East Alligator
River, NT* MORRIS
LEFT INSET: *Intermediate egret* MORRIS
RIGHT: *Post wet grasses, Nourlangie Creek,
NT* MORRIS

COME, LET us praise the Lord!
  Let us sing for joy to God, who
    protects us!
Let us come before him with
    thanksgiving
  and sing joyful songs of praise.
For the Lord is a mighty God,
  a mighty king over all the gods.
He rules over the whole earth,
  from the deepest caves to the
    highest hills.
He rules over the sea, which he
    made;
  the land also, which he himself
    formed.

Come, let us bow down and
    worship him;
  let us kneel before the Lord, our
    Maker!
He is our God;
  we are the people he cares for,
  the flock for which he provides.

PSALM 95:1–7

LEFT: *East coast, Tas* MORRIS
UPPER RIGHT: *Ayers Rock, NT* SPIKER
LOWER RIGHT: *Igalkal Swamp, East Alligator area, NT* MORRIS

YOUR WORD is a lamp to guide me
　and a light for my path.

PSALM 119:105

I LOOK to the mountains;
　where will my help come from?
My help will come from the LORD,
　who made heaven and earth.

He will not let you fall;
　your protector is always awake.

The protector of Israel
　never dozes or sleeps.
The LORD will guard you;
　he is by your side to protect you.
The sun will not hurt you during
　　the day,
　　nor the moon during the night.

The LORD will protect you from all
　　danger;
　he will keep you safe.
He will protect you as you come
　　and go
　now and for ever.

PSALM 121

Lord, you have examined me
    and you know me.
You know everything I do;
    from far away you understand
        all my thoughts.
You see me, whether I am
        working or resting;
    you know all my actions.
Even before I speak,
    you already know what I will say.
You are all around me on every
        side;
    you protect me with your power.
Your knowledge of me is too deep;
    it is beyond my understanding.

Psalm 139:1–6

To be wise you must first have reverence for the Lord. If you know the Holy One, you have understanding.

Proverbs 9:10

UPPER LEFT: *Giant water lily, Kakadu, NT* MORRIS
LOWER LEFT: *Koala* SPIKER
RIGHT: *Red-eyed tree-frog* MORRIS

T HE DESERT will rejoice,
   and flowers will bloom in the
      wastelands.
The desert will sing and shout for
      joy;
   it will be as beautiful as
      the Lebanon Mountains
   and as fertile as the farmlands
      of Carmel and Sharon.
Everyone will see the LORD's
      splendour,
   see his greatness and power.

Give strength to hands that are
      tired
   and to knees that tremble with
      weakness.
Tell everyone who is discouraged,
   'Be strong and don't be afraid!
   God is coming to your rescue,
   coming to punish your enemies'.

The blind will be able to see,
   and the deaf will hear.
The lame will leap and dance,
   and those who cannot speak
      will shout for joy.
Streams of water will flow
      through the desert;
   the burning sand will become a
      lake,
   and dry land will be filled with
      springs.

ISAIAH 35:1–7

BACKGROUND: *The Three Sisters, Blue
Mountains, NSW* MORRIS
LEFT: *Hay bales, South Gippsland, Vic* SPIKER
RIGHT: *Woolleybutt blossoms* MORRIS
OVERLEAF: *Early morning, Pyrenees Ranges,
Vic* SPIKER

THE LORD said, 'Sing for joy, people of Jerusalem! I am coming to live among you!'

ZECHARIAH 2:10

J OHN APPEARED in the desert, baptising and preaching. 'Turn away from your sins and be baptised', he told the people, 'and God will forgive your sins'. Many people from the province of Judea and the city of Jerusalem went out to hear John. They confessed their sins, and he baptised them in the Jordan River.

John wore clothes made of camel's hair, with a leather belt around his waist, and his food was locusts and wild honey. He announced to the people, 'The man who will come after me is much greater than I am. I am not good enough even to bend down and untie his sandals. I baptise you with water, but he will baptise you with the Holy Spirit.'

MARK 1;4–8

LEFT BACKGROUND: *Marron grass* SPIKER
UPPER LEFT: *Arnhem Land stream,*
NT MORRIS
RIGHT: *Spinifex hillside, Wittenoom Gorge,*
WA MORRIS

A T THAT time the Emperor Augustus ordered a census to be taken throughout the Roman Empire. When this first census took place, Quirinius was the governor of Syria. Everyone, then, went to register himself, each to his own home town.

Joseph went from the town of Nazareth in Galilee to the town of Bethlehem in Judea, the birthplace of King David. Joseph went there because he was a descendant of David. He went to register with Mary, who was promised in marriage to him. She was pregnant, and while they were in Bethlehem, the time came for her to have her baby. She gave birth to her first son, wrapped him in strips of cloth and laid him in a manger — there was no room for them to stay in the inn.

There were some shepherds in that part of the country who were spending the night out in the open, taking care of their flocks. An angel of the Lord appeared to them, and the glory of the Lord shone over them. They were terribly afraid, but the angel said to them, 'Don't be afraid! I am here with good news for you, which will bring great joy to all the people. This very day in David's town your Saviour was born — Christ the Lord! And this is what will prove it to you: you will find a baby wrapped in strips of cloth and lying in a manger.'

Suddenly a great army of heaven's angels appeared with the first angel, singing praises to God:

'Glory to God in the highest
    heaven,
and peace on earth to those with
    whom he is pleased!'

LUKE 2:1–14

A CHILD is born to us!
    A son is given to us!
    And he will be our ruler.
He will be called, 'Wonderful
        Counsellor',
    'Mighty God', 'Eternal Father',
    'Prince of Peace'.

ISAIAH 9:6

LEFT: *Giant water lilies, Magela Creek, Kakadu, NT* MORRIS
RIGHT: *View from the top of Mt Kosciusko, NSW* MORRIS

NOT LONG afterwards Jesus came from Nazareth in the province of Galilee, and was baptised by John in the Jordan. As soon as Jesus came up out of the water, he saw heaven opening and the Spirit coming down on him like a dove. And a voice came from heaven, 'You are my own dear Son. I am pleased with you.'

At once the Spirit made him go into the desert, where he stayed forty days, being tempted by Satan. Wild animals were there also, but angels came and helped him.

MARK 1:9–13

LEFT BACKGROUND: *Chitchester Range National Park, WA* MORRIS
LOWER LEFT: *Perentie, Ormiston Gorge, NT* MORRIS
RIGHT: *Devil's Pebbles, Tenant Creek, NT* MORRIS

JESUS SAID:

'Happy are those who know
  they are spiritually poor;
 the Kingdom of heaven
  belongs to them!
'Happy are those who mourn;
 God will comfort them!
'Happy are those who are humble;
 they will receive what God
  has promised!
'Happy are those whose greatest
  desire
 is to do what God requires;
 God will satisfy them fully!
'Happy are those who are
 merciful to others;
 God will be merciful to them!
'Happy are the pure in heart;
 they will see God!
'Happy are those who work for
  peace;
 God will call them his children!
'Happy are those who are
  persecuted because they do
  what God requires;
 the Kingdom of heaven belongs
  to them!'

MATTHEW 5:3–10

UPPER LEFT: *Floodplain frog* MORRIS
LOWER LEFT: *Female satin flycatcher* SPIKER
RIGHT: *Coppery brushtail possum, Crater National Park, Qld* MORRIS

THIS, THEN, is how you should
    pray:
'Our Father in heaven:
    May your holy name be
        honoured;
    may your Kingdom come;
    may your will be done on earth
        as it is in heaven.
    Give us today the food we
        need.
    Forgive us the wrongs we have
        done,
        as we forgive the wrongs that
        others have done to us.
    Do not bring us to hard
        testing,
        but keep us safe from the Evil
        One.'

MATTHEW 6:9–13

LEFT: *Ghost gum* SPIKER
RIGHT BACKGROUND: *Arafura Sea,
NT* MORRIS
RIGHT INSET: *Great egret, Darwin
Harbour, NT* MORRIS
OVERLEAF: *Old wagon, Alice Springs,
NT* SPIKER

ESUS CHRIST is the same
yesterday, today, and for ever.
HEBREWS 13:8

J *ESUS SAID:* 'Come to me, all of
you who are tired from carrying
heavy loads, and I will give you rest.
Take my yoke and put it on you,
and learn from me, because I am
gentle and humble in spirit; and
you will find rest. For the yoke I will
give you is easy, and the load I will
put on you is light.'

J ESUS SAID: 'Once there was a man who went out to sow grain. As he scattered the seed, some of it fell along the path, and the birds came and ate it up. Some of it fell on rocky ground, where there was little soil. The seeds soon sprouted, because the soil wasn't deep. But when the sun came up, it burnt the young plants; and because the roots had not grown deep enough, the plants soon dried up. Some of the seed fell among thornbushes, which grew up and choked the plants. But some seeds fell in good soil, and the plants bore grain: some produced a hundred grains, others sixty, and others thirty . . .

'Listen, then, and learn what the parable of the sower means. Those who hear the message about the Kingdom but do not understand it are like the seeds that fell along the path. The Evil One comes and snatches away what was sown in them. The seeds that fell on rocky ground stand for those who receive the message gladly as soon as they hear it. But it does not sink deep into them, and they don't last long. So when trouble or persecution comes because of the message, they give up at once. The seeds that fell among thornbushes stand for those who hear the message; but the worries about this life and the love for riches choke the message, and they don't bear fruit. And the seeds sown in the good soil stand for those who hear the message and understand it: they bear fruit, some as much as a hundred, others sixty, and others thirty.'

MATTHEW 13:3–8, 18–23

RIGHT BACKGROUND: *Cane fields, Tully, Qld* SPIKER
UPPER INSET: *Gomphrena during fire, East Alligator area, NT* MORRIS
LOWER INSET: *Varied lorikeet, Arnhem Land coast, NT* MORRIS

54

ONE DAY Jesus got into a boat with his disciples and said to them, 'Let us go across to the other side of the lake'. So they started out. As they were sailing, Jesus fell asleep. Suddenly a strong wind blew down on the lake, and the boat began to fill with water, so that they were all in great danger. The disciples went to Jesus and woke him up, saying, 'Master, Master! We are about to die!'

Jesus got up and gave an order to the wind and the stormy water; they died down, and there was a great calm. Then he said to the disciples, 'Where is your faith?'

But they were amazed and afraid and said to one another, 'Who is this man? He gives orders to the winds and waves, and they obey him!'

LUKE 8:22–25

UPPER BACKGROUND: *Traditional Indonesian vessel, Ashmore Reef, WA* MORRIS
UPPER LEFT: *Reef fish* MORRIS
LOWER RIGHT: *Storm clouds near Lake Cargellico, NSW* SPIKER
UPPER RIGHT: *Handover ceremony, Uluru National Park, NT* MORRIS

ESUS LOOKED around and saw that a large crowd was coming to him, so he asked Philip, 'Where can we buy enough food to feed all these people?' (He said this to test Philip; actually he already knew what he would do.)

Philip answered, 'For everyone to have even a little, it would take more than two hundred silver coins to buy enough bread'.

Another one of his disciples, Andrew, who was Simon Peter's brother, said, 'There is a boy here who has five loaves of barley bread and two fish. But they will certainly not be enough for all these people.'

'Make the people sit down', Jesus told them. (There was a lot of grass there.) So all the people sat down; there were about five thousand men. Jesus took the bread, gave thanks to God, and distributed it to the people who were sitting there. He did the same with the fish, and they all had as much as they wanted. When they were all full, he said to his disciples, 'Gather the pieces left over; let us not waste any'. So they gathered them all up and filled twelve baskets with the pieces left over from the five barley loaves which the people had eaten.

JOHN 6:5–13

JESUS TOOK with him Peter, James, and John, and led them up a high mountain, where they were alone. As they looked on, a change came over Jesus, and his clothes became shining white — whiter than anyone in the world could wash them. Then the three disciples saw Elijah and Moses talking with Jesus. Peter spoke up and said to Jesus, 'Teacher, how good it is that we are here! We will make three tents, one for you, one for Moses, and one for Elijah.' He and the others were so frightened that he did not know what to say.

Then a cloud appeared and covered them with its shadow, and a voice came from the cloud, 'This is my own dear Son — listen to him!' They took a quick look around but did not see anyone else; only Jesus was with them.

MARK 9:2–8

BACKGROUND: *Wet season sunset, East Alligator River, NT* MORRIS
RIGHT INSET: *MacDonnell Ranges, Simpson's Gap, NT* MORRIS

The TEACHER of the Law wanted to justify himself, so he asked Jesus, 'Who is my neighbour?'

Jesus answered, 'There was once a man who was going down from Jerusalem to Jericho when robbers attacked him, stripped him, and beat him up, leaving him half dead. It so happened that a priest was going down that road; but when he saw the man, he walked past on the other side. In the same way a Levite also came along, went over and looked at the man, and then walked past on the other side. But a Samaritan who was travelling that way came upon the man, and when he saw him, his heart was filled with pity. He went over to him, poured oil and wine on his wounds and bandaged them; then he put the man on his own animal and took him to an inn, where he took care of him. The next day he took out two silver coins and gave them to the innkeeper. "Take care of him", he told the innkeeper, "and when I come back this way, I will pay you whatever else you spend on him".'

And Jesus concluded, 'In your opinion, which one of these three acted like a neighbour towards the man attacked by the robbers?'

The teacher of the Law answered, 'The one who was kind to him'.

Jesus replied, 'You go, then, and do the same'.

LUKE 10:29–37

BACKGROUND: *The Olgas, NT* MORRIS
RIGHT INSET: *Old work boot* SPIKER

J ESUS SAID: 'There was once a man who had two sons. The younger one said to him, "Father, give me my share of the property now". So the man divided his property between his two sons. After a few days the younger son sold his share of the property and left home with the money. He went to a country far away, where he wasted his money in reckless living. He spent everything he had. Then a severe famine spread over that country, and he was left without a thing. So he went to work for one of the citizens of that country, who sent him out to his farm to take care of the pigs. He wished he could fill himself with the bean pods the pigs ate, but no one gave him anything to eat. At last he came to his senses and said, "All my father's paid workers have more than they can eat, and here I am about to starve! I will get up and go to my father and say, 'Father, I have sinned against God and against you. I am no longer fit to be called your son; treat me as one of your paid workers'." So he got up and started back to his father.

'He was still a long way from him when his father saw him; his heart was filled with pity, and he ran, threw his arms around his son, and kissed him. "Father", the son said, "I have sinned against God and against you. I am no longer fit to be called your son." But the father called to his servants. "Hurry!" he said. "Bring the best robe and put it on him. Put a ring on his finger and shoes on his feet. Then go and get the prize calf and kill it, and let us celebrate with a feast! For this son of mine was dead, but now he is alive; he was lost, but now he has been found".'

LUKE 15:11–24

RIGHT BACKGROUND: *Western MacDonnell Ranges, NT* SPIKER
UPPER INSET: *Crops south of Burra, SA* SPIKER
LOWER INSET: *Hereford cattle, Kangaroo Valley, NSW* MORRIS

SOME PEOPLE brought children to Jesus for him to place his hands on them, but the disciples scolded the people. When Jesus noticed this, he was angry and said to his disciples, 'Let the children come to me, and do not stop them, because the Kingdom of God belongs to such as these. I assure you that whoever does not receive the Kingdom of God like a child will never enter it.' Then he took the children in his arms, placed his hands on each of them, and blessed them.

MARK 10:13–16

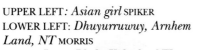

UPPER LEFT: *Asian girl* SPIKER
LOWER LEFT: *Dhuyurruwuy, Arnhem Land, NT* MORRIS
RIGHT: *Jamey Blyth, Kakadu, NT* MORRIS

THE LARGE crowd that had come to the Passover Festival heard that Jesus was coming to Jerusalem. So they took branches of palm trees and went out to meet him, shouting, 'Praise God! God bless him who comes in the name of the Lord! God bless the King of Israel!'

Jesus found a donkey and rode on it, just as the scripture says,
'Do not be afraid, city of Zion!
Here comes your king,
riding on a young donkey.'

His disciples did not understand this at the time; but when Jesus had been raised to glory, they remembered that the scripture said this about him and that they had done this for him.

JOHN 12:12–16

LEFT: *Donkeys, Turkey Creek, WA* MORRIS
RIGHT BACKGROUND: *Pandanus tree* MORRIS
RIGHT INSET: *Arnhem Land students collecting edible palms* MORRIS
OVERLEAF: *Sunset at Marla, SA* SPIKER

WHILE THEY were eating, Jesus
took a piece of bread, said a prayer
of thanks, broke it, and gave it to
his disciples. 'Take it', he said, 'this
is my body'.

Then he took a cup, gave thanks to
God, and handed it to them; and
they all drank from it. Jesus said,
'This is my blood which is poured
out for many, my blood which seals
God's covenant. I tell you, I will
never again drink this wine until
the day I drink the new wine in the
Kingdom of God.'

MARK 14:22–24

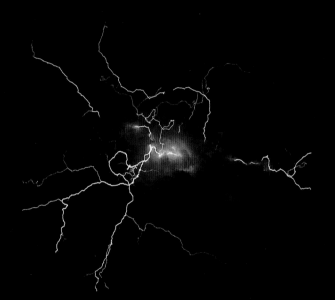

IT WAS nine o'clock in the morning when they crucified him. The notice of the accusation against him said: 'The King of the Jews'. They also crucified two bandits with Jesus, one on his right and the other on his left . . .

At midday the whole country was covered with darkness, which lasted for three hours. At three o'clock Jesus cried out with a loud shout, *'Eloi, Eloi, lema sabachthani?'* which means, 'My God, my God, why did you abandon me?' . . .

With a loud cry Jesus died.

The curtain hanging in the Temple was torn in two, from top to bottom. The army officer who was standing there in front of the cross saw how Jesus had died. 'This man was really the Son of God!' he said.

MARK 15:25–27,33,34,37–39

LEFT: *Electrical storm over East Alligator, NT* MORRIS
UPPER RIGHT: *Old stump* SPIKER
LOWER RIGHT: *Sunset, the Olgas, NT* SPIKER

H E ENDURED the suffering that
 should have been ours,
 the pain that we should have
  borne.
All the while we thought that his
 suffering
 was punishment sent by God.
But because of our sins he was
 wounded,
 beaten because of the evil we did.
We are healed by the punishment
 he suffered,
 made whole by the blows he
  received.
All of us were like sheep that were
 lost,
 each of us going his own way.
But the Lord made the punishment
 fall on him,
 the punishment all of us
  deserved.

ISAIAH 53:4–6

LEFT: *Mangrove roots, East Alligator River,
NT* MORRIS
RIGHT: *Sunset, East Alligator River, NT*
MORRIS

ERY EARLY on Sunday morning the women went to the tomb, carrying the spices they had prepared. They found the stone rolled away from the entrance to the tomb, so they went in; but they did not find the body of the Lord Jesus. They stood there puzzled about this, when suddenly two men in bright shining clothes stood by them. Full of fear, the women bowed down to the ground, as the men said to them, 'Why are you looking among the dead for one who is alive? He is not here; he has been raised. Remember what he said to you while he was in Galilee: "The Son of Man must be handed over to sinful men, be crucified, and three days later rise to life".'

Then the women remembered his words, returned from the tomb, and told all these things to the eleven disciples and all the rest.

LUKE 24:1–9

LEFT: *The Olgas, NT* SPIKER
RIGHT: *Near Alice Springs NT* SPIKER

THE ELEVEN disciples went to the hill in Galilee where Jesus had told them to go. When they saw him, they worshipped him, even though some of them doubted. Jesus drew near and said to them, 'I have been given all authority in heaven and on earth. Go, then, to all peoples everywhere and make them my disciples: baptise them in the name of the Father, the Son, and the Holy Spirit, and teach them to obey everything I have commanded you. And I will be with you always, to the end of the age.'

MATTHEW 28:16–20

WHEN THE apostles met together with Jesus, they asked him, 'Lord, will you at this time give the Kingdom back to Israel?'

Jesus said to them, 'The times and occasions are set by my Father's own authority, and it is not for you to know when they will be. But when the Holy Spirit comes upon you, you will be filled with power, and you will be witnesses for me in Jerusalem, in all of Judea and Samaria, and to the ends of the earth.' After saying this, he was taken up to heaven as they watched him, and a cloud hid him from their sight.

They still had their eyes fixed on the sky as he went away, when two men dressed in white suddenly stood beside them and said, 'Galileans, why are you standing there looking up at the sky? This Jesus, who was taken from you into heaven, will come back in the same way that you saw him go to heaven.'

ACTS 1:6–11

LEFT: *East Alligator River, NT* MORRIS
CENTRE: *The Grampians, Vic* SPIKER
RIGHT: *Oncoming storm-clouds* SPIKER

WHEN THE day of Pentecost came, all the believers were gathered together in one place. Suddenly there was a noise from the sky which sounded like a strong wind blowing, and it filled the whole house where they were sitting. Then they saw what looked like tongues of fire which spread out and touched each person there. They were all filled with the Holy Spirit and began to talk in other languages, as the Spirit enabled them to speak . . .

About three thousand people were added to the group that day. They spent their time in learning from the apostles, taking part in the fellowship, and sharing in the fellowship meals and the prayers.

ACTS 2:1–4,41,42

LEFT BACKGROUND: *White tern* MORRIS
LEFT INSET: *Wind-blown tree on the Nullarbor, WA* MORRIS
RIGHT: *Paperbark fire, East Alligator River, NT* MORRIS
OVERLEAF: *Dawn ceremony, Galiwinku, NT* MORRIS

S AUL KEPT up his violent threats of murder against the followers of the Lord. He went to the High Priest and asked for letters of introduction to the synagogues in Damascus, so that if he should find there any followers of the Way of the Lord, he would be able to arrest them, both men and women, and bring them back to Jerusalem.

As Saul was approaching the city of Damascus, suddenly a light from the sky flashed around him. He fell to the ground and heard a voice saying to him, 'Saul, Saul! Why do you persecute me?'

'Who are you, Lord?' he asked.

'I am Jesus, whom you persecute', the voice said. 'But get up and go into the city, where you will be told what you must do.'

The men who were travelling with Saul had stopped, not saying a word; they heard the voice but could not see anyone. Saul got up from the ground and opened his eyes, but could not see a thing. So they took him by the hand and led him into Damascus. For three days he was not able to see, and during that time he did not eat or drink anything.

ACTS 9:1–9

W E KNOW that a person is put right with God only through faith in Jesus Christ, never by doing what the Law requires. We, too, have believed in Christ Jesus in order to be put right with God through our faith in Christ, and not by doing what the Law requires.

GALATIANS 2:16

I T IS BY God's grace that you have been saved through faith. It is not the result of your own efforts, but God's gift, so that no one can boast about it.

EPHESIANS 2:8,9

LEFT: *Wet night on William Street, Sydney, NSW* MORRIS
RIGHT BACKGROUND: *Morning sun, Dunolly, Vic* SPIKER
RIGHT INSET: *The barred window, storehouse, Hermannsburg, NT* SPIKER

S HOULD WE keep on sinning so that God's grace will increase? Certainly not! We have died to sin — how then can we go on living in it? For surely you know that when we were baptised into union with Christ Jesus, we were baptised into union with his death. By our baptism, then, we were buried with him and shared his death, in order that, just as Christ was raised from death by the glorious power of the Father, so also we might live a new life.

ROMANS 6:1–4

LEFT: *Birdwing butterfly, Cairns, Qld* MORRIS
UPPER RIGHT: *Red Lily Plains, East Alligator River, NT* MORRIS
LOWER RIGHT: *Water lilies, Waterfall Creek, NT* SPIKER

WE KNOW that the Law is spiritual; but I am a mortal man, sold as a slave to sin. I do not understand what I do; for I don't do what I would like to do, but instead I do what I hate. Since what I do is what I don't want to do, this shows that I agree that the Law is right. So I am not really the one who does this thing; rather it is the sin that lives in me. I know that good does not live in me — that is, in my human nature. For even though the desire to do good is in me, I am not able to do it. I don't do the good I want to do; instead I do the evil that I do not want to do . . .

What an unhappy man I am! Who will rescue me from this body that is taking me to death? Thanks be to God, who does this through our Lord Jesus Christ!

ROMANS 7:14–19,24,25

BECAUSE OF God's great mercy to us I appeal to you: Offer yourselves as a living sacrifice to God, dedicated to his service and pleasing to him. This is the true worship that you should offer. Do not conform yourselves to the standards of this world, but let God transform you inwardly by a complete change of your mind. Then you will be able to know the will of God — what is good and is pleasing to him and is perfect.

ROMANS 12:1,2

CHRIST IS like a single body, which has many parts; it is still one body, even though it is made up of different parts. In the same way, all of us, whether Jews or Gentiles, whether slaves or free, have been baptised into the one body by the same Spirit, and we have all been given the one Spirit to drink.

For the body itself is not made up of only one part, but of many parts . . .

If one part of the body suffers, all the other parts suffer with it; if one part is praised, all the other parts share its happiness.

All of you are Christ's body, and each one is a part of it. In the church God has put all in place.

1 CORINTHIANS 12:12–14, 26–28

I MAY BE able to speak the languages of human beings and even of angels, but if I have no love, my speech is no more than a noisy gong or a clanging bell. I may have the gift of inspired preaching; I may have all knowledge and understand all secrets; I may have all the faith needed to move mountains — but if I have no love, I am nothing. I may give away everything I have, and even give up my body to be burnt — but if I have no love, this does me no good.

Love is patient and kind; it is not jealous or conceited or proud; love is not ill-mannered or selfish or irritable; love does not keep a record of wrongs; love is not happy with evil, but is happy with the truth. Love never gives up; and its faith, hope, and patience never fail.

Love is eternal.

1 CORINTHIANS 13:1–8

LEFT: *Smith Point, Cobourg Peninsula, NT* MORRIS
UPPER RIGHT: *Rainbow lorikeet feeding on apple blossoms, NSW* MORRIS
CENTRE RIGHT: *Bustard, Hall's Creek, WA* MORRIS
LOWER RIGHT: *Wheel of fire tree, NSW* MORRIS

THE TRUTH is that Christ has been raised from death, as the guarantee that those who sleep in death will also be raised . . .

Listen to this secret truth: we shall not all die, but when the last trumpet sounds, we shall all be changed in an instant, as quickly as the blinking of an eye. For when the trumpet sounds, the dead will be raised, never to die again, and we shall all be changed . . .

Then the scripture will come true: 'Death is destroyed; victory is complete!'
    'Where, Death, is your victory?
    Where, Death, is your power to
        hurt?'

Death gets its power to hurt from sin, and sin gets its power from the Law. But thanks be to God who gives us the victory through our Lord Jesus Christ!

1 CORINTHIANS 15:20, 51,52, 54–57

LEFT: *Canopus butterfly* MORRIS
UPPER RIGHT: *Sandstone fig leaf* MORRIS
LOWER RIGHT: *Wedge-tailed eagle* MORRIS

F REEDOM IS what we have —
Christ has set us free! Stand, then,
as free people, and do not allow
yourselves to become slaves
again . . .

What I say is this: let the Spirit
direct your lives, and you will not
satisfy the desires of the human
nature . . .

The Spirit produces love, joy,
peace, patience, kindness,
goodness, faithfulness, humility,
and self-control. There is no law
against such things as these. And
those who belong to Christ Jesus
have put to death their human
nature with all its passions and
desires. The Spirit has given us life;
he must also control our lives.

GALATIANS 5:1,16, 22–25

YOU REMEMBER that ever since you were a child, you have known the Holy Scriptures, which are able to give you the wisdom that leads to salvation through faith in Christ Jesus. All Scripture is inspired by God and is useful for teaching the truth, rebuking error, correcting faults, and giving instruction for right living.

2 TIMOTHY 3:15,16

SINCE CHRIST suffered physically, you too must strengthen yourselves with the same way of thinking that he had; because whoever suffers physically is no longer involved with sin. From now on, then, you must live the rest of your earthly lives controlled by God's will and not by human desires . . .

My dear friends, do not be surprised at the painful test you are suffering, as though something unusual were happening to you. Rather be glad that you are sharing Christ's sufferings, so that you may be full of joy when his glory is revealed. Happy are you if you are insulted because you are Christ's followers; this means that the glorious Spirit, the Spirit of God, is resting on you.

1 PETER 4:1,2, 12–14

UPPER LEFT: *Agile wallaby* MORRIS
LOWER LEFT: *Blue-billed duck* SPIKER
RIGHT: *Cave plants, Arnhem Land, NT* MORRIS

DEAR FRIENDS, let us love one another, because love comes from God. Whoever loves is a child of God and knows God. Whoever does not love does not know God, for God is love. And God showed his love for us by sending his only Son into the world, so that we might have life through him. This is what love is: it is not that we have loved God, but that he loved us and sent his Son to be the means by which our sins are forgiven . . .

God is love, and whoever lives in love lives in union with God and God lives in union with him.

1 JOHN 4:7–10, 16

I LOOKED, and I heard angels,
thousands and thousands of them!
They stood around the throne, the
four living creatures, and the
elders, and sang in a loud voice:
  'The Lamb who was killed is
      worthy
    to receive power, wealth, wisdom,
      and strength,
    honour, glory, and praise!'

And I heard every creature in
heaven, on earth, in the world
below, and in the sea — all living
beings in the universe — and they
were singing:
  'To him who sits on the throne
      and to the Lamb,
    be praise and honour, glory and
      might,
    for ever and ever!'

The four living creatures answered,
'Amen!' And the elders fell down
and worshipped.

REVELATION 5:11–14

BACKGROUND: *Sunset, Magela Creek,
Kakadu, NT* MORRIS
FAR LEFT: *Red-collared lorikeet* MORRIS
NEAR LEFT: *Sugar glider* MORRIS
NEAR RIGHT: *Jewel beetle, NT* MORRIS
FAR RIGHT: *Snapping turtle, NT* MORRIS
OVERLEAF: *Dry season smoke haze, Kakadu,
NT* MORRIS

THEN I SAW a new heaven and a
new earth. The first heaven and the
first earth disappeared, and the sea
vanished. And I saw the Holy City,
the new Jerusalem, coming down
out of heaven from God, prepared
and ready, like a bride dressed to
meet her husband. I heard a loud
voice speaking from the throne:
'Now God's home is with human
beings! He will live with them, and
they will be his people. God himself
will be with them, and he will be
their God. He will wipe away all
tears from their eyes. There will be
no more death, no more grief or
crying or pain. The old things have
disappeared.'

REVELATION 21:1–4

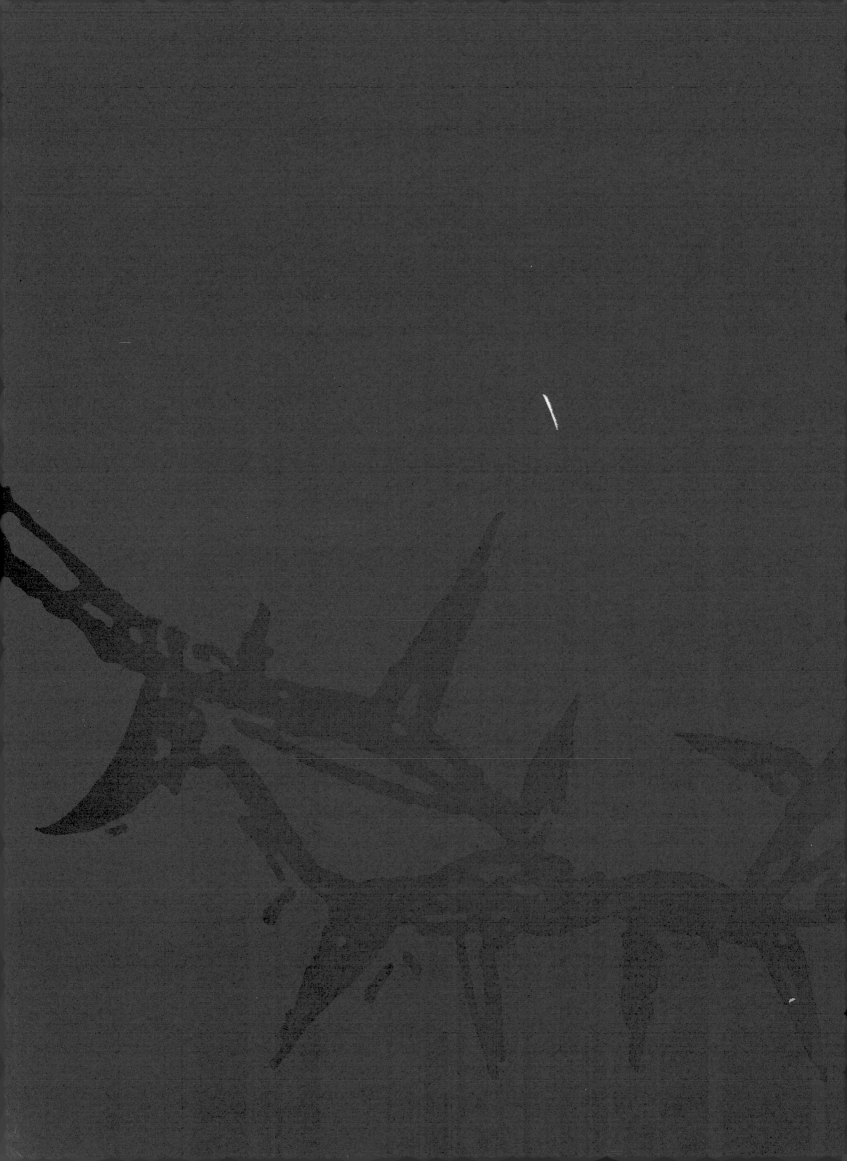